# AT THE CONSULA HOTEL

# AT THE CALIGULA HOTEL

*and other poems*

## Brian Aldiss

SINCLAIR-STEVENSON

First published in Great Britain in 1995
by Sinclair-Stevenson
an imprint of Reed Consumer Books Ltd
Michelin House, 81 Fulham Road, London SW3 6RB
and Auckland, Melbourne, Singapore and Toronto

A CIP catalogue record for this book
is available at the British Library

ISBN 1 85619 568 6

Typeset by Deltatype Ltd, Ellesmere Port, Cheshire
Printed and bound in Great Britain by
Cox & Wyman Ltd, Reading, Berkshire

for
dearest Tim and Helen
on their momentous journey

# Acknowledgements

No, I Was Never Deaf or Blind to Her Music, from *Brothers of the Head*. London: Pierrot Publishing, 1977.

Boars Hill: the Sycamores and the Oaks, in the *Boars Hill Newsletter*, 1988.

The Twentieth Camp in *P.E.N. New Poetry II*, edited by Elaine Feinstein. London: Quartet Books, 1988.

Fragment of a Longer Poem from *Barefoot in the Head*, Faber & Faber, 1969.

At the Caligula Hotel (from sequence Homage to the Early Pound), in *Science Fiction Blues Programme Book*. London: Avernus, 1987.

Short Stories from *A Tupolev Too Far*, HarperCollins, 1993.

What Did the Policeman Say?, in *Philip K. Dick Society Newsletter*, 1992.

Mary in Italy in *Keats-Shelley Review*, autumn 1990.

Rice Pudding, in *Now We Are Sick*, edited by Neil Gaiman & Stephen Jones. Minnesota: DreamHaven Books, 1991.

Lunar Anatomy (as Lunar Astronomy) in *Colours of a New Day*, edited by Sarah Lefanu & Stephen Hayward. London: Lawrence and Wishart, 1990.

Found, from *Farewell to a Child*, Priapus Poets, 1982.

Destruction of the Fifth Planet, in *Star\*line 5*, 1982.

Femalien, in *Science Fiction Blues*, Avernus, 1988.

Thomas Hardy Considers the Newly-Published Special Theory of Relativity, in *The Times Literary Supplement*, 25th September 1982.

'Rhine Locks are Closed in Battle against Poison', in *Science Fiction Blues Programme Book*. London: Avernus, 1987.

The Cat Improvement Company, in *Science Fiction Blues*. London: Avernus, 1988.

The Expanding Universe, in *Science Fiction Blues*. London: Avernus, 1988.

To a Triceratops Skull in the British Museum, in *Science Fiction Blues*. London: Avernus, 1988.

The Light, in *The Magazine of Speculative Poetry*, April/June 1987.

Flight 063, in *Asimov's Science Fiction*, 1994.

Alphabet of Ameliorating Hope, from *A Tupolev Too Far*, HarperCollins, 1993.

# Contents

# I Imagery?

# At the Caligula Hotel

The dew is on the leaf, darling,
    And they are playing Ravel's 'Bolero'.

'How can one endure nights without music?'
    She asks; but we are being precious.
'Oh, darling,' – sighs in the ineffectual
    Moonlight – 'how hungry I am . . .'
*More caresses, or a chicken dansak?*
    Like many a heart-mad lover, I
Settle for the lesser thing.
    After all, the lady's always willing,
While even Indian restaurants close
    At midnight, moon or no moon.

The dew is on the leaf
    And they are playing Ravel's 'Bolero'.

*Sweet is the music of a breaking papadum.*

# Chinese Exercises

## *Lu Tai*

Of course I could tell you of Lu Tai
Who hates to go to bed alone.
She is not the cleverest or the fairest
  And her little dog roots up my salvias:
But ah, when Lu Tai has her limbs about you
It could rain cucumbers for all I care.
For the sake of Lu Tai's golden kisses
  The young Buddha would forswear archery.

## *Nocturne*

All day the mare cropped amid the buttercups
As I waited by the slanting tree.
  At the seventh hour music sounded:
  Men brought their hooks to reap the green of May.
Tired of watching me wander through my rooms
The night burst forth in thickets of lilac
While the stars that sank in the river
Showed up dancing at my windows.
  She whom I love dreamed of a creaking stair
  To wake with my hand on her shoulder.

## *Interval*

Poised on a stone statue
My grey falcon deliberates
The great green wheel stops turning
A thousand ages burn like palaces

### Indecision

In winter my mother's house is cold
She sits all day and gazes at the Wo Tung River
Hardly dares cough for fear of noise
   Every day I mean to send her a letter
   Why can we never say
   The necessary words?
Why does frost scrawl such elaborate flowers
Upon the barrier of her window pane?

### Journeying

Chestnut trees accompany our climb up the mountain
Stop the carriage and let us look back
What countries we have left behind, what fields, what
                                 towns
   What warm hands of those once friends
   Because of a single gesture nineteen years ago
Now darkness comes down in a faded blue shawl

### Poems from a Later Dynasty III

### Who Hears My Voice?

   Twice a day the sun rests on the horizon
The mad cannot distinguish dusk from dawn.
Youth has gone and left only a wilderness
In which hang trophies of remote partings and beds.
Outside, dusk garners in the birds;
Lighting one pale candle in my hut
Eclipses the whole grey bulk of Mount Fy Lai.

   Beyond Fy Lai stand range on range of mountains.
The third watch sounds, I cannot look towards them.
Moonlight on a slate roof, hard as justice.
Little by little the night turns round,
Velvet and inviolate on its stoney axis.
Back come the words of other dynasties:
Thoughts infest the hollow spaces.

Golden toads already gnaw the eastern quarter.
Help me, O my brothers. I thought I heard satin wings
And tasted the lips of her who brought eternity.
In my dishonoured room the silence thickens.
No message ever came after my friends' coaches left.
Beauty that shakes a kingdom has broken my cornerstone.
Who hears my voice, my footstep on the flags?

*B.W.A. and Li Shang-Yin*
*April 976–1976*

# Exit Aquascutum

By the time I decided to wake,
She had left for her teaching job.
Her clothes were strewn across the floor
Like children's paintings. Well, we weren't

Exactly made for one another.
'You're so unfashionable!' she'd said.
I had a fixation about the permanent;
She was mad about the transitory.

   Outside, the air was inhospitable
   And I had arrived without my coat.

# While Feeding Parrots, November 9th

'No, of course there's no one else . . .'
    Does she believe me? Her brow clears,
She smiles, she does believe. And I?
    I believe my words but not my fears.

Oh, if she only knew how much and by how far
    She was the only one! She would not ask
Ever again, or even love me more,
    Feeling unequal to the task!

# Winter Bites Deep

*– composed from headlines in* The Independent *Saturday 18th
& Sunday 19th December 1993*

WINTER BITES DEEP INTO THE HEART OF OLD
REPUBLICS

YOU HAVE TO LET THEM BE FREE TO DIE –

ALL BRANCHES OF THE FAMILY.

    THE CITY CAN'T CONTINUE IN SPLENDID ISOLATION

BEAUTIFUL, USEFUL AND OVERBLOWN.

A NEIGHBOUR ROTS ON THE SEVENTH FLOOR

A LONG DAY ON THE CAPITALIST ROAD

A LITURGY SET IN HISTORICAL TIME –

AN A TO Z OF HELL.

    DIRTY WORK, BUT SOMEONE'S GOT TO DO IT

MANY ARE CALLED BUT FEW STICK IT OUT.

A BETTER DEAL FOR SOME THAN OTHERS . . .

# Breughel's Hunters in the Snow

The freeze continues. There's little to put in the pot.
They don't speak. An hour more and darkness will fall.

They're weary, and made all the wearier
By their lack of success.
Perhaps they'll have a drink at the inn
Before trudging home to confess
It's going to be bread and salt again.
Winter's not much of a time.

Father was never one to complain.
Once he was past his prime
He merely became unsociable
As if he was one of the hunters in the snow.
He'd say when we went out anywhere,
'Let's hope we don't meet anyone we know' —
As though a word might give him away.
Mother became pretty silent too.
When you came home empty-handed
You'd keep your trap shut, wouldn't you?

# Anau: The Well

Beyond the mulberry trees
Before the mosque    Beside the huts
Our guides lift up the wooden trap

Down beneath the clarity of the surface
Sand and fresh-water shrimps curl
The bucket falls, is hauled up dripping

Of course I'd had advice
I thought of all the warnings but I drank
Drank the cool waters of Turkmenistan

Beside the huts    Before the mosque
Beyond the mulberry trees    Beneath whatever skies
I think of all the warnings and I drink

# The Cynar, Istanbul

An unknown hotel, night thoughts all slack
And lack of sleep about say 2 a.m.

Pulling back the curtains I step out
Into a warm euphoria. All seems calm.
And there before my sight, unguessed, the moon
Full-faced gleams down upon the Sea of Marmora.

# Dawn in Kuala Lumpur

The avenue yields up its fumes by starlight,
Unpeeling wrappings layer by layer.
No leaf but harbours something of tomorrow.
   No time-checks, please, and not an uttered prayer.

Be circumspect! The smiling next-door neighbours
Prise up your floorboards when the night bat flies.
Your acts are heirlooms. Neon's dimly burning.
   Moonlight stains the shutters of closed eyes.

And those who come like lovers in their sandals
To imitate the gestures of the past
Will fill their street with anybody's banners:
   Repentance slows. Dawn waits. Her breath comes fast.

Delight is scarcely longer than a letter.
Disgust's a library. And yet –
The intellect's the boards on which treads folly
   And flesh the stage on which the play is set.

This city once knew dawns of livid splendour.
Pollution now rags out the sky in grey.
Do men who rise and shower and drive to office
   Know their lives have been processed away?

Is feeling then a gateway to disaster
Or is it sense that signals us to doom?
The eye, that carnivore, eats what it rests on,
   The ape invades the drawing-room.

Impatience follows swiftly on the act.
Pay up, and face the suckling light alone!
What have we next, replacing secret night?
   Bent backs, false fronts, memos, the phone . . .

For those of us who sleep in nature's doorways
And shut our pockets to society's bills
The stones are cheeks whereon we rest our temples –
   Meanwhile, the city crawls towards the hills.

Some ghosts may through night's banyan thickets filter
But waking finds a world still upside down.
The map we rescued from the gutters
   Proved street plan to some other town.

I heard a footfall in the smallest hour.
When starting up I thought I saw a face;
But to my challenge came the solemn answer:
   'I'm here but you are in another place.'

And much as hope may serve as sail and anchor
The sea is hourly storming up the strand.
The candle gutters in the widow's window.
   Preserve your heart. Permit me but your hand.

New-born, the sun, at mosque and supermarket
Proclaims that day's the flower of midnight's seed.
The Muslims pray. The rest of us rise up
   To spend that common coin of human need.

# Gauguin's Tahiti

As a kingfisher flashed from the lagoon,
Cynar splashed along the foreshore in the evening tide,
    And all its wild sky ride
Swaggered with atmospheric blues and greens.
Sunset, as no man else had dared to conjure,
Swallowed a new-born moon, and rolled towards the hut
    Wherein that great nude slut
Stared at occultly decorated screens

Behind the bed. Whereon, as on the screens,
Her man lay drugged, body turned olive like the night.
    Upon the woman's right
Her beaten bronze bowl stood stacked high with fruit,
Fruit that waxed luminous as flesh decayed,
Fish-fruit, fox-fruit, to make your lips curl back afraid –
    Fruit like a fear delayed –
Yet in dreams densely denizened the brute

Abed had gorged himself upon her flesh.
The painter cruelly caught them just before they died:
    The sunset in its pride,
The man in lechery, and in the room
Viridians of evil. So the seer
Inside the poet and the devil in the saint
    Achieve the power to paint
Invisible but all-encroaching doom,

To warn and warn that one night, all we've been
Will be the dust of nothing, and what life we saw
        But patterns on a screen.
To warn and warn that one night, never more –
As in the drownings of a fevered dream –
To light and warm us, down will sink the lurid sun
    Beneath its seas, and none
Will see us more upon this passionate shore.

# II  Everyday?

# No, I was Never Deaf or Blind to Her Music

No, I was never deaf or blind to her music
I breathed more oxygen in her company
Reached higher speeds and a wider sort of skies
And dredged for her secret salts and alkalis

It was just that the days closed in
A new motorway went up between her place and mine
We couldn't agree on the merits of Stockhausen
She got funny about my friends too
We stopped going to concerts
And then there was that business with her sister
    Never properly explained
And she grew lousy about apologising
She said she lost her respect for me when I couldn't give up
                                                    smoking

But no, I was never impervious to her vistas
Plunging into the lake of what she was
She stormed me every day like valiant deeds
And my head was as full of her as poppy seeds

It was just that the weather changed
My job took me up to Sheffield every week
I felt a compulsion to join the Scientologists
She got mad on bringing stray cats home
We started watching television
Then there was the problem with global pollution
    Surely could have been prevented
And I sat and watched her body disintegrating
Felt what was smooth turn into kipple
    I longed for our time again

No, I was never deaf or blind to her music
Time was, her alchemy was all upon me
She packed every moment like a picnic box
She was air and sea to my hills and rocks
I was never deaf or blind to her music

# Toledo: Three Ladies

Far inland the stones are dry and intricate.
Here where the Holy Office once held court
Japanese tourists gather tidily
To view the Assumption of Count Orgaz
Before the light goes. Before the light goes
Here's another famous city lingered in
For all of four point five hours
Another later-to-be-fabulous meal
Consumed between the Iglesia de los Reyes
And the Muslim synagogue.
                                        Isobel
Exiled Jews and Conversos, hungry for
Gold and purer faith and blood. Whereon
Her country crumbled into such decline
It now needs tourists flown from East and West
To restock treasuries and monuments.
There's little moral to be gained from this
The past is not a textbook of morality.
Both Saint Teresa of Avila and
Torquemada were of mingled race.
Holy Juan de la Cruz probably Converso was
Imprisoned here.
                              Two ladies show me Spain
One greedy and one frugal. One bestows
Lunch and an antique clock then hurries off.
The other lady later writes a verse
Under the influence of Chinese poetry
And water. Age means living far inland
Youth is a troubled sea.

# Government

Listen to the politicians
Kissing superior arse
Guarding their positions
Being Upper Class
Condescending to the Lower
Spreading monetary damnation
Trading principle for power
Ruining the nation
Speaking with a lying tongue
Massaging all the figures
Shutting out the hopeful young
Still thinking Blacks are 'niggers'

Selling up the Welfare State
Closing down the clinics
Opening the doors of hate
Turning us to cynics
Converting value into cash
Mistaking poverty for crime
Prompting us to something rash —
Like flushing out this rotten slime

# Moonglow: for Margaret

Past midnight. In our wilderness we still have hopes to tame,
I walked alone through moonglow pure as water, thoughts
                                                        alight
With visions of your dearness, Margaret. At length there came
To musing mind that time when you and I — however bright
The round-eyed moon — will tend these lawns no more.
Then in our children's hearts perhaps a calm
Night air may resurrect us, and restore
Us to our garden, two ghosts arm-in-arm.

Would Plato, and the wise who conjure better worlds, conceive
Such images of perfect forms, had Earth no sister sphere
Immune in silver? Does this binary condition leave
Its imprint on each passing human pair, or interfere
With history in sly sublunar ways?
Would I have been with so much joy undone,
Say, if you did not light my darkling days
And walk with me, through bright moonlight or none?

# Alfie Cogitates on Life

'Well, of course it's a four-letter word,'
Says I, with my usual humour –
I'm known for my usual humour –
'LIFE. Its meaning's a sort of a con trick –
There's just days and there's years. It's a rumour
To claim like there's any *connection*
Between 'em, put out by some bloke
In some university.' Honest,
I think as the whole thing's a joke,

A load of old highbrow-type crap.
Here I'm set with two kids and a wife –
The boys and my common-law wife –
When a mate what I works with says 'Alf,
What the hell do you make of this Life?'
Says I, 'There's just days and there's years,
Chum' – I really was telling him flat –
'You get born, you have kids, you're a goner . . .
There's bugger all meaning in that.'

# Memories of Palić

Were you ever in Palić?
— Supposing somebody asked
Today —
Behind the simple Yes I'd give would be
That whole grand setting of park and icy lake
And a palace that once had seen Hungarian lords
In all their glory. Cranes now nested on their roofs.

The lights and the taps didn't work in our room, and the paths
Went unswept, so that last year's leaves found their way to our
door,
Rattling and crunching along the marble stair,
While our shuttered windows gazed towards the frontier post.

Across the soggy lawns we walked, to find
A *gostiona* where the evenings passed
To shrill *czigany* music, Palić wine,
And songs of Smederevo or lost love.

Glasses smashing in the grate —
*Pesme*, *igre*, lust and hate
Sorrow, choler,
In a *kola* . . .
Faster, more, a
Slow lament
From *Crna Gora*.

Remember how we met two travellers, both
War's victims, how he'd journeyed overland
From Hong Kong. How they waited while his bank
Negotiated currencies and laws . . .

In its frosty stillness the winter sought to hold
The year against invader Spring, and life
And yet — and yet we had our foreign warmth
To quicken in the slow-pulsed corridors.

Were you ever in Palić?
– Supposing somebody asks
Today! –
I would passionately answer, 'Yes, and not alone!'
A fair girl was with me who walked those unswept paths,
Who sang those songs and slept with me in that room,
Listening to leaves. Though time has passed, she's with me still.

And by that unmelting lake our ghosts still go,
Well-wrapped among the dim Slavonic limes,
Heeding the ancient music,
Unaware
That *pro tem* warmth between us was to prove *večan*.

# Boars Hill: the Sycamores and the Oaks

The sycamores sway. And what they say may be translated
thus:
'Boars Hill was old when this ancient wold was covered with
alder and oak,
When the boars still dropped their litters that cropped the
tender bracken muss.
Boars fought with their tusks in the Oxfordshire dusks when
the hunters came to soak
The leaves and the ground for yards around with the blood
of both sow and mate;

Those leather men were remorseless then, but they somehow
arrived too late.
They arrived too late, for the boars all ate the last of the
acorns still.
So the oaks became rare, there was space to spare – that's
when *we* slipped up the Hill.'

The oak trees creak. And what they speak may be
translated so:
'When the sycamores, those tramps and whores, slipped in to
seize our room,
We oaks were bound to stand our ground where custom bid
us grow,
For we truly hate such a profligate. It spells our doom
As its endless seeds spring up like weeds which choke away
the light.
But the Boars Hill folks could defend us oaks if they'd only
up and fight
To cleanse their land and their houses grand with a
systematic kill
Of the sycamores – aren't you sick of yours? – then we'd save
our lovely hill!'

# All Things Transfigure

All things transfigure in the mind,
The known is wrapped in mystery,
The Other turns out otherwise.
To land, a ship is freedom's self —
The land the same in sailors' eyes.

The guilt that brands our human kind
Was once an infant innocence.
Since secrets cry themselves aloud,
How then, my love, is it with you?
Is only hate with tongue endowed?

Though two's an even number, we're
Ever at odds, poor transient pair,
And each step forward leads us back —
As if I was a foe who gains
By my advances your attack.

If our love's a refuge, now a jail
Houses your versifier turned
Your adversary, deeds are mud,
The English rose has bitter thorns,
The milkmaid wants her pint of blood.

That 'all' I gave you was, it seems,
Not quite enough to mend a shoe,
And what you gave I simply stole.
All Men are mortal save ourselves —
Or did we dream we once were whole?

Poor broken things, let's contemplate
If this is what fulfillment means,
If without Faith our faithlessness
Is natural, and nature not
So different from unnatural mess.

Then could you not surrender, love,
And by so doing conquer me?
Set disobedience in revolt:
Give up your claim of faultlessness
And I shall find in you no fault.

You are the darling of my day,
The demon of my waking thought.
All that was mine you undermined;
The kiss once kindling now is ash,
All things transfigure in the mind.

We cast out God — to fill his place
With devils, and in crowded hearts
Pack emptiness. Foresight was blind,
Yet our paired hopes need not despair:
All things transfigure in the mind.

Let shut be open, open shut —
Convert yourself, throw wide the door,
Be my beloved — no more knocks!
All things transfigure in the mind —
Like married bliss, that paradox.

# Trapped in the Present

Not a sound inside and not a star
Without. The darkness comes at five o'clock
And never misses. No one speaks or calls.
Am I then dead? The novel does not live.
Surviving through another hour needs all
My strength. Its minutes bore like woodworm through
The timbers of my flesh. No sound outside.
Trapped in the present, I – but knowing well
The future is a shore of deeper night.

# The Path

O Lord, I reach the gateway of old age.
        Look upon me.
As I stand now at your draughty forecourt
        Look upon me
In my bewilderment. Preserve in me
A late ambition to be wise. Forgive
My sins, my cowardice, my blindness. Save
Me from a righteous rage to denigrate
Those follies which I once myself enjoyed.
Lend me support to aid me on my way
To that more dreadful gate I have to go
Through, unafraid, whenever you decide.

O Lord, in whom I've sought to disbelieve,
        Look upon me,
Fortify an atheist's lack of faith.
        Look upon me,
Greyer, older, that as faculties
Decay and fade I shed my self-regard.
Lord, take this burden of my character
Away I've shouldered all my years. At last
I near the final step. Then may I make
No special claims, that all those whom I love
May not by fears be shamed – remembering
They too must travel down the path I tread.

# Suburban Sunday

*The roses make our room amazing,*
*Safe behind its double-glazing.*

French cricket on the narrow lawn;
A bike-ride by the old canal
Which sinks in mist at summer's dawn;
A curry at the 'Taj Mahal'.

The fish farm where a trout was bought;
Syringa perfuming the street;
The thrush we saved the cat had caught;
The pub, with friends we chanced to meet.

*Neighbours want to be acquainted*
*Now the house has been repainted.*

No style, originality,
Or pace informed our long weekend.
Yet happiness sat in our tree
And sang to make the whole world mend.

The bud can never know the rose;
We in our origins rejoice –
Our leafy Oxford's June repose
Murmurs with Eden in its voice.

*Day dwindles – yet how light it is!*
*And supper is crab sandwiches . . .*

# Nature Notes: Early September

Beetle, while I watch you,
Busy, armoured, bright,
　Are you aware
That this noonday sun
Will give way to night?

　The jay knows so much.
　It hides in the Japanese maple
　Communing with distance.

　　Clouds slide over silver birches.
　　Trees: You move fast without sound.
　　　Relax and try the warm ground.
　　Clouds: We're too majestic to hustle.
　　　And it's vulgar to rustle.
　　Trees: We're enjoying the sun.
　　　Why be rude to us?
　　Clouds: We're fair weather cumulus:
　　　We make the world run.

　　　Already on the nondescript rose
　　　　On our sunniest bank
　　　Brilliant red hips deepen
　　　And blackberry blacker grows.
　　　　Seasons steepen
　　　　Towards autumn.

The mellow brick of the house
Has known eighty summers
And is warm to the hand,
Articulate.
The dragonfly is new,
Flashy, computerised,
Won't speak or wait.

Silence makes this midday hour
Bright and tensioned like a flower.

The sky, the sun, the woods,
    Count these multitudes!
The sun, the woods, the sky.
    Such rich diversity!
The woods, the sky, the sun.
        These multitudes are one!

These days I live on wine and water
    With birdsong for litany.
Marking her sixteenth year, my daughter
    Is cycling in Brittany.

The laurels glitter like teeth,
Always immaculate,
Unaware of folly.
They grow taller than apple trees,
Neater than holly,
Greener than verdigris.

        Plants in the conservatory
        Growing by brick and glass.
            Silent house guests,
            Letting life in,
            Letting it pass.

Easy, fly, settling on my arm!
What's this haste of yours?
Don't you understand leisure?
Stop and listen to my blood –
There, there under your paws –
Feel its slow pleasure.

        Lean Macramé's a huntress
        On the veldt of the lawn.
        She has just caught, killed, and torn
        A shrew as big as a lioness.

A small white feather on the grass.
  Now it rests in my hand.
Once it was part of flight.
Once this day was night.
  What do I understand?
  What do I understand?


The ground falls away,
Greensand over clay,
Into copse and dell
Towards Sunningwell.
The skyline jumps
To Wittenham Clumps.
One can certainly say
The ground falls away.


Nothing moves in the heat.
  A bird sings.
Nothing moves in the heat.
  A leaf trembles.
Nothing moves in the heat.
  A cat twitches.
Nothing moves in the heat.
  Silence complete.


  Well, the war for today is done
    And the rodent 'Last Post' sounded.
  The Cats as usual have won,
    Dragging in their dead and wounded.


There are several toads in the neighbourhood.
Their lives are wise and slow and good.
They squat in your palm like a gift bestowed,
  Skin rough and cool,
  Eye bright as jewel.
But only a slug would pray to a toad.

A tiny cat skull lies beached
Like a shell under the pines.
Between the delicate tines
Of bone a snail has reached
Sanctuary in an optic cave.
What was once fast of sight,
Quick of paw, light,
Now is lethargy's slave.

The sun looks into all our open windows,
Creating patterns on the patterned carpets.
It is so slow about its work today
The sunset may be subject to delay.

The grasses laugh when they grow.
The Japanese knotweed is solemn,
Thinking lustful thoughts of pollen.
Knotweed spreads but does not know
Throughout the galaxy the squitches
Keep a million planets in stitches.

# Willow Cottage

Here in my exile, lurid amber light
Seems to embalm the day as if no flight
Of fancy could imagine night,
As if the swing of sun across
The fields were pendular. No loss
To me if in its arc of burn
The orb should reach that ragged hedge, then turn
And soon regain the eastern apple trees –
Only to pause once more, as if in thought,
To pause, and then with supernatural ease,
Bounce back: above the dazzled meadows caught,
An undecided exile in this peace,
Like me a vessel with an unmapped port.

That lurid amber light, how it deceives!
For all the while it seems to drench near leaves
And distant hills with an eternal glow,
Time tunnels yet: and in the world of men –
That city where I was a citizen –
The hours are marked, the shops are closed,
Lamps lit. It's later far than I supposed.
I look up from my paper, when
I find my room drowns in a pool of dark,
The writings die, they die upon the page . . .
Only outside, against the leaden lawn,
The skies bear brightness from some earlier age
When nights and partings were unknown.

This must be dusk, or is it dawn?
Is daylight being born, or is it dead?
Another of my stock of days has fled,
And I sit musing here alone.

Ah friends, and those who shed some thought
Upon me in this place – ah, friends, some sport
Of nature sends me nights as fraught
With magic as the days, as deep
In silence and the stealthy tread of time.
So moòns that lure away all hope of sleep
And stars that in the blue-mouthed heavens ring
Sleep's knell awake the characters I bring
To book. They sally forth to fill my world,
To do great deeds of love, or its reverse,
To go down to the dead, to kiss or curse.
And all this while the universe, unfurled
Before my window, slants upon its course!
While galaxies speed blazing through the sky
Like zeppelins aflame. I know that days
Go by – what's in that to amaze?
But here I know I know the days go by.

# Cold Snap

No mercy in nature and none in the train
We die as we travel by halts and degrees
Snow cannot cover – it skimps round the trees
Where's the iron frost, so blood can freeze.

Blow, wind, bring the kind of extremes
Necessity needs
Like our dreams
The windows are clogged with our breath

A well-wrapped boy walks the playing field
But where are the starving
And those who appealed
To the CAB for a fiver for heating.
Bare branches of course, birds dying
Snow drifting, sleet lying –
Yet it's all so fleeting
What's a cold snap for
When the passengers sit reading their papers
About some distant war that doesn't bleed them?
They're going to their mortgaged homes
Smug bankers, drapers, lechers, lecturers.
Where's the frost to bite foot and hand
The potato eaters, the scroungers for coal,
The iron hard river
The old brought out on stretchers?
Bend down Siberia to see Europe clystered
Empty the bowl
Make the middle class feel
The Romantic ideal of the Sublime
The extreme, the bitter, and the blistered,
The heart's North Pole,
The bite of blight to the brain.

No mercy in nature – and none in the train

# Stoney Ground

Christ chose a hard and stoney road:
All preaching, little social whirl,
Too driven ever to settle down
With some nice Jewish girl.
Or was it choice? It's hard to know.
At Canaan, with the wedding planned,
Turning the water into wine,
Does he too get pretty canned?

Or share that gift – so well worth owning –
In Gethsemane at night
On Saturdays, to have a ball
With Peter and his other chums?
When he saves the whore from stoning,
Does he get a free fuck off her,
Up against the Wailing Wall,
Till with joy Our Saviour comes?

Or was he one, so great on talk,
Whose life is inwardly dead loss,
No girls, no booze, no fun – and so
As well to end up on the Cross?

# The Triumph of the Superficial

Here sprawls Delice, as pretty as she's proud,
Trite as her secrets are when named aloud.

This is the curse that silences the crowd:
Trite are their secrets all when said aloud.

This is why sinners to their priests stay bowed:
Trite all their sins become, confessed out loud.

This is why dead men moulder, safe in shroud.
Trite would their secrets be if whispered loud.

This is why love had best stay unavowed –
Trite are its hopes when hotly mouthed aloud.

So, my Delice, I stand before you, cowed.
Trite are my secret lusts when cried aloud.

# The Twentieth Camp

*for Elaine Feinstein*

All the centuries were on display across the plain,
Each closely guarded, wired, and separated from the next.
And yet, despite the dogs and floodlights, people made their
way
Beyond the barricades, going in fear and fugitive,
Each subject to inherited blind promptings to survive.

Inside these gulags stretching to infinity we saw —
And did not cease to marvel as we looked — how every one
Contained a circumscribed diversity of love and hate.
The strikers and the struck, the givers and the ones who took,
Praying or cursing, some forsaken, others who forsook.

A fearful beauty in the camps prevailed. Some folk
maintained
A gentle air throughout all punishment. Among the eyes
That challenged us, dark in their violence, a few there were
Which shone compassion: men and women who, behind their
bars
Immured, sustained a spirit almost free. Yet all bore scars.

When to the largest of these fearsome camps we came, we
cried,
'How is it that this Twentieth brims with so much despair,
Much more oppression, famine, war, and mouths stopped in
their prime?'
The answer came: 'Your knowledge without wisdom cannot
save,
And Man, enslaving all of nature, is himself a slave.'

# Good Fortune

The gipsy's eyes
Seemed to penetrate through my disguise.
She treated me like a man and said,
'You will be free when some are dead.
Then you'll pay some visits overseas
And there you'll meet a maid to please,
Tall and fair and not a tease.
*Though your back will break*,
She will never once cause your heart to ache.

Dear, buy this charm.'
So I pressed a shilling into her palm –
Pocket money quickly spent –
And came out of the seaside tent
Only to find my parents waited
There, all hot and agitated,
Shouting at me, irritated,
'You waste your precious cash!
That old gipsy woman has sold you trash.'

Did I see through
That odd fortune-telling act? How true
Became the deeds that day foretold?
Well, some are dead and I am old,
And many visits I have paid
To foreign places. Once, delayed,
I met a tall and pleasing maid ...
*My back is still all right*,
And that lady has soothed me many a night.

The world of sense,
Of streets, computers, dividends,
Has ruled out superstitious things:
God lurks no longer in the wings,
And who cares what the stars foretell?
It's 'market forces' ring our knell;
We're on our own, for ill or well.
I keep the silver charm
That the gipsy pressed into my palm.

# Communication

I stood on the veldt one night
Watching colours as deep as a sea,
Unable to sleep for joy.
   While I radiated light
   A figure appeared to me
   Half-animal, half-boy

And it waved like a god aflame.
I thought it was in my head
And not on the dusty track.
Next day my neighbour came:
'I waved to you,' he said.
'Why didn't you wave back?'

# A Summery Meditation on Money

The spring-backed frogs
disinterestedly fuck
in a green cool
    June brings elderflowers
each like a galaxy on stalks
I move towards them
brushing leaves and light-years
from my legerdemained face

My brother conducts himself
like music in a neat column
pensively

    A picture of Jannick Storm
interleaved in Rodovre
between photography and his son
or driving into the restless ochre
of Copenhagen

Czars are still riding on tramcars
we fall in love in crowded streets
whatever the season time is here to stay
and money-matters
not unpleasing to my mind
after all
everything has a value

    Late in a purple July night
I lie and listen to distant traffic
the roses are rude and ragged
both children and lawns grow brown
our clocks tick indicating
nothing but Sunday
some of the cars bear off prams and boats and luggage
making like raiders for the coast
our trees stand still as mountains

        Round us
the roses are rude and ragged
paint of blue in my fingernails
'Somebody re-painted the sky,' I tell
my little son. Who says 'They went
all over the clouds.
The birds won't know how to fly!'
I gaze across at the chest-of-drawers
an antique growing in value
like the whole world tonight

        Remember a graffito glimpsed
on an old Oxford wall
THE WELL-ROGERED MIND
KNOWS NO DISCONTENT
It's a family man's revelation
that blood is money's blood-relation

        Summer's so mercenary
        sounds go further
        we plan to fly away
        in a flutter of travellers' cheques
        green means leaves and money

Friends, love baseness
don't scorn everything but purity
whatever the season
crime is here to stay
we're all bastards
hogging the well-rogered life
bless the sun on your pimply back
and the heat of pox in your blood
pink's for kids – green's the oldest
colour of oceans and Martians
involved in wicked primaeval
revolutions of earth
green the stalk and green the scale
grey brains still pay green its danegeld

It's only one captivity
among a million
in our warmth
transactions
coupled-up sunlight
permeates pockets
Tiepolo forgeries
corruscate
Later the rude highwayman
autumn
as the last flower dies from the crossroads
will call us to account

Man invented debt
time and minaret
as the czars rattle into the freedoms of sleep
the dime is here to stay
whatever the season
there's credit yet.

# A Moment of Suspense

In the ginger field
Two young stallions
One black one white
Frisk like an animated Stubbs

In our sedate pines
Last of what were extensive woods
The wind howls
On its way to Bristol

In this moment
With all its terraces
And immense cycles
Everything lasts forever

# Fragment of a Longer Poem

One day I shall walk ahead
up certain sunken steps into a hall
patterned with tiles in black and red
and recognise the colour and the place
as well as if I once went back
in time up certain shallow sunken steps
and came into a hall with black
and red tiles in a certain memorised
pattern that makes me think I tread
up sunken steps into a hallway and
confront a tiled floor patterned red
and black which forces me to think I stand
before some steps whose sunken tread
leads on into a hall whose patterned tiles

# III  Literary?

# Short Stories

When someone in the audience asked how
I saw my short stories, I offered them
Antarctica. The ice shelf grinding
Forward with the century
Carrying freights of fossil Bronze Age snow
Until a thousand flaws united.
Then with huge mammalian groans
The burdened stone thing calved.

You know (I told my listeners, hoping
They might), those icebergs there are frequently
Over a hundred kilometres long –
As big as Monte Carlo. Solemnly
They drift beyond the Weddell Sea
Like Matterhorns breasting the South Atlantic.
Riding out gales shaved by the wind and warmth
Heading north for Rio and Capricorn.

But as they're sighting the Malvinas
They suffer the environment
These old cathedrals of the cold
Have shrunk. They'd go into your gin
And tonic. So they're lost to human ken
But for some months they have a real existence
And scientists keep tabs on them.
They're mad and lovely while they last.

That's how (I told the audience)
I see my stories. They formed part of me.
Those who sight them in those desolate
Latitudes of publishing sometimes
Are awed. They praise a colour
Or an unexpected shape.
They seldom hear the groans of birth.
A year, a year, and they are gone.

   The audience clapped uncertainly.
   Then asked if I kept office hours.

# What Did the Policeman Say?

*In Memoriam PKD*

What was it in the USA
That cast a shadow on the brightest scenes
So that even creativity
Needed its massed amphetamines?
What did the policeman say?

And what's on Ganymede today? –
That Entity which, cunning in its snare,
Destroys our hopes for any constancy
In love. Amid the world's despair
What did the policeman say?

Supposing friends should fade away
And what seems Truth unveil itself as Lie?
When simulacra rule, whom should we blame
For all the rerum lacrimae?
What did the policeman say?

What irony makes fame delay,
Or fortune dawdle till the hour is late?
Beware! An ashen hostile Presence breeds
Corruption in the Golden State.
What did the policeman say?

An end to questioning and fears
Comes when we're numbered with the dead –
Or will there be more cause for 'Flow my tears' –
Just as the policeman said.

Our hold on life has little stay.
And at the closure of our tragic masque
When we confront the error of our ways,
We'll have but little need to ask
What did the policeman say,
What did the policeman say?

# Hamlet Folk

They do little, the people of Elsinore,
Courtiers, cooks, or soldiers at the castle.
One in a thousand may have seen a ghost.
When they move, soft-booted, it's in crowds
As if rehearsed. They're somewhat less than kin
And more like kine. They always face the front,
Glad of a madness or some royal tiff,
Applaud or boo – but not too much,
Fading behind a handy battlement.
Even their clothes are indeterminate:
Medieval-Edwardian, like their food,
All sucking pig and plastic chicken.

They have no home-life, only entrances,
So children never caper through the throng.
These are shadows who have lost their scripts
And consequently have no inner life.

They're onlookers at the drama of the king,
Subjects who bow as Hamlet passes
Cloudy with his fate. Mortality
Is on his mind. He sees his lines will lead
To bloody eminence. Soliloquies
Give way to swords. The carnage comes.
The citizens stand back for Fortinbras,
Tidy as sheep. Death passes them
Without a glance, greedy for blood, for life,
For those familiar with their sentences.

# The Poor

When Cowper was sitting at his Dereham desk
Contemplating a poem without rhyme –
Wearing that turban Romney painted –
He saw the poor as merely picturesque,
Enjoying an Eighteenth Century rustic time.
    This view was already antiquated.

Came Marx! And now the poor were seen in chains,
Slaves to *Das Kapital* and avarice.
So half the world rose up and in alarm
Murdered its monarchies and brighter brains:
Installing instead dystopian paradise,
    Terror, gulag, collective farm.

Came 1991! Lenin and Marx
And all the systems grounded in their lore
Now proved bankrupt – a mere outmoded mess.
They fell, swift as Kalashnikov round barks.
Democracy at last! At last the poor
    Were free to suffer, imageless . . .

# On Reading Poetry in Berkhamsted

Very few turned up. The poet cursed.
The wind that marched through Hertfordshire
Has kissed Siberia first,
And lingered then through Europe, on its way
Picking up chills from lunar craters,
Ice-green VDUs, teeming refrigerators.
So no great crowd among the library books
Jostled to hear the man who read
'On Reading Poetry in Berkhamsted'.

Very few turned up. The poet wept.
To celebrate his life he staged
An orgy while he slept
Wherein all the girls who ever tempted
Him should come from east and west –
And naturally the south. Streets emptied
But the girls went elsewhere. Very few turned up
Or stripped to please the man who read
'On Reading Poetry in Berkhamsted'.

Very few turned up. The poet died.
Parson, widow, sister, sexton –
Alone they testified
– And raised a stone and read a text on –
This man once paid his tax and VAT
And read his Salman Rushdie dutifully.
This was the final blow of all:
They held a funeral – and few turned up
To weep upon the man who read
'On Reading Poetry in Berkhamsted'.

Very few turned up. The poet felt decomposed.
The wind that moved through Hertfordshire
Was none too well disposed.
Greenhouse effect, pollution, and
Broached ozone layer brought up to the boil

A crisis in grave ecologic terms
Which sterilised the Berkhamstedian soil.
So very few turned up among the worms
Who came to feed upon the man who read
'On Reading Poetry in Berkhamsted'.

# Poem Inspired by Scott Meredith

Back in the days of oil lamps
You could strap a pack on your back
And cross any frontiers

Back when the steam trains ran to Truro
Butterflies blew like curtains
Through poppy-decked wheatfields

When I could jump our garden fence
I knew a girl proud as an eagle
And kissed her in our kitchen

You must forgive my melancholy
Now I'm just an ageing writer
Who's had to sack his agent.

# Two Painters

## *I Francis Bacon*

Caught in the sumptuous deadly scarlet room
    Of bare existence
The bilious boneless male ejaculates
    At some expense
The cardinal behind his private glass
    Practices screaming
Horror the painter says is all our ration
    The rest's seeming
Even innocent quadrupeds are caught
    In the bog
Festering staring out in apprehension
    Like Goya's little dog

## II Fernand Khnopff

You will remember the unruly beating
Of the heart in the throat. The breath constricted
That something more than love you bore your sister
Your ghostly images of something less than happiness
Dreams, silence, hair, and *femmes fatales*
Burne-Jones and Schopenhauer and Socialism
A century crumbling to its end.

When wandering through Bruges the other day
I saw the dead city through your eyes
Despite the ice cream parlours
*Bruges-la-Morte* among its old canals
Still drowns in your reflections.
What charcoal and pencil once created
Proves more powerful than stone.
The god of sleep who held you by the hand
Wakes me to see how I contrived
A freer life than you. In my portfolio
*My Heart Does Not Cry for the Past*
I reverence your symbolism and
Those closed interiors – yet never can
*I Lock My Door Upon Myself*

Remember the stale mornings and the mists
Sappho in half-completed pastel
Waistcoats, shadows, opium
And the shuttered bedroom windows

# Light of Ancient Days

A romantic sense of something too remote
For memory to reach: but this for sure,
The clothes they wore were all hand-sewn, the house
Pillared amid its garden, sanctified,
And she we see, stage left, was virginal
To such degree the bourbon rose she plucks
Won't scratch her skin.
                            The very title tells
Us much, 'Enchanted Gardens' – set no doubt
Somewhere between Giotto's Italy
And Stanley Spencer's Cookham. 'Look ye here,
What I intended was a beautiful –'
The artist's voice speaks to my inner ear –
'Romantic dream of all that never was
And never will be'. Stillman was his name,
Died 1912. I try to intervene:
He says in sulky tone, 'You realist,
You Burne-Jones hater, look upon the light
Suffusing all, the house, the gracious dames,
The sward whereon they tread. That is the light
Which smacks of ancientry, more pure than shone
Ever on any land or sea.' 'I like
The light, admittedly,' I said, 'so why
Should all your ladies – and this little page –
Look wan and limp, with less expression than
My cat?' 'It's *myth*. This is a place that none
Can reach – only desire.' 'Yet here desire
Is dead.' 'You're no Romantic,' Stillman quoth.
'You shall not buy my oil, you philistine.'

# Mary Shelley, 1816

Oh, Willmouse, what am I writing?
Can you not see how the rain comes down?
It's so dramatic and yet deadly.
The surface of the lake seems like to drown
Its own pocked face. Your little world
Is summerless – but you're my sun.
I sing the progress that will sweep
Away our monarchies, our ignorance . . .
I sing for you . . . And yet a secret thing
Towers over us, all monstrous, with a deep
Sense of its injury – oh that, Willmouse,
I'm doing well . . . Live, little angel, sleep,
Wake – and I'll be here, rain or no rain,
Still giving all my milk and love –
Still working, as I try to plumb
Our living mysteries, the phantasms
That plague us. Do you see the dark
A-lurking at the stairwell, sweet,
Spreading like ink-stains on this sheet?

Willmouse, what am I writing?

# Victor Frankenstein on the Mer de Glace

The surface is uneven, mimicking
Waves of a troubled sea. Two hours it takes
To cross. And this great frozen river winds
Among dependent mountains hid in cloud.

He came at me with superhuman speed,
Too fast, too large, and too malign. I watched
The spectre born of my ambition rush
Out from his frozen mother, halt, and speak.

'I am thy creature, spurn me not. Enjoy
My intercourse till sunset. Misery
Has made me fiend. I have allied myself
With nature's deserts, wombed in caves of ice,

Away from monarchies and learning's courts,
Thy exiled Adam – though from Nature's pulse
Expelled. Am I the tongue of many-voiced
Ravines of power that garbs itself in rock

Of caverns inaccessible and pines –
Those children of an earlier time – with whose
Columns the tempests play? Was thy intent
O Frankenstein, to fashion me the voice

Of all allied to homelessness? The wolf,
The eagle sailing to Blanc's very summit . . .
Even the snow, the lightning bolt, know more
The joys of kinship than do I, alone.

Yet all these elemental forces here
Combined – lakes, forests, peaks and ravaged cliff –
Offer sweet comfort set beside thy heart.
You icy father, know you not of love?'

His tumbling cataract of speech came down
Upon me. 'By my striving I had hoped
To win the love and worship of all men,
And to repeal large codes of woe. Instead,

By my unnatural act I am undone,
By your malignancy I also bear
The brand of exile. Whether I am just
Or not, begone, devil, insect, away!'

He smiled, and from his broken purple lip
Steam issued. 'Then, creator, we are one
In this at least: one in the fires of wrath,
One in the winter of the world's cold hate.'

I followed him. Had any looked on us
They would have thought us kin, and fallen back
Aghast. But none there was. We were the last
Of earth. I followed him toward his lair.

# The Shelleys

## – To a Lady who spoke of their 'Mystery'

I know no mystery about the Shelleys
Who speak to us across the years direct –
At least as clearly as the dead can talk
To those who, on the right side of the grave,
Pursue each other, or the Truth. Percy
The vegetarian perceived his world
In clear dualities: a charnel house
From which might rise like glorious insects winged
Perceptions, messengers of future time,
Spreading their beauties to a better age.
And what of Mary? Shy, retiring, cool,
And ever faithful to her husband's name
When he with all his faithlessness was gone.
From the tormented child to widowhood
Was but a decade: in that time she snatched
Out of a wet ungenial summer such
A tale! It in its dark prophetic tones
Lives on, long after she who gave it birth
Has passed away. Her *Frankenstein* retains
Its spell and all it spelt. The mystery lies here,
In that invention which, as Mary said,
Is born from chaos, not a void, and gives
To dark and shapeless substances a form.

So from that teeming summer by the lake
Where poets talked or wrote away the hours,
The silent Mary spoke. And told a tale
Addressing those mysterious fears which haunt
Our nature. Shelley drowned, and Mary died.
I know no mystery about the Shelleys.
About invention – that's another thing . . .

# The Created One Speaks

Through a world of glaucomas
I move like a flock of birds
With timed co-ordinations –
A plurality of a being

Tell me who are these unexplained children
And the deaths of which I am compounded.
All lie like silt stirred up by thought
Within the millrace of my being.
Phantasms of an older world
Like ruins of dead empires rise
To haunt my sleep. Forgotten men
Sutured within me discompose
My waking – or is all a dream
A product of the mothering dead?

So I shun the tortuous world of men
To seek the ringing spaces of the north
The unconstructed cold, the unparsed pole.
And after me pursuing runs one Man
Maker and breaker of the natural law
Who growing closer also grows more like.

# Mary in Italy

Shelley's conception of love was exalted,
Absorbing, allied to all that is purest
In our nature, and warmed by passion.
No poet ever expressed the gentler
Or more forcible emotions of the soul
In such heart-rending fashion.

He lit the dark of life with sympathy and love:
Perfectly amiable, he dreamed of human liberty.
He died, and the world showed no outward sign.
Yet his influence is fast augmenting
In England and in Italy – whither I go now –
Where his aspirations mingled with mine.

The evening was most beautiful when I arrived.
The horned moon hung in the light of a sunset
That threw a glow as from some grander world
Over the track along which I strived,
Over the piney mountains and the deep valleys distantly
                                          ranged.
I will not pursue Buffon's sublime but gloomy theory
That this globe which we inhabit
Will at some future period be changed
Into a frozen pebble. All will be lost
In the encroachments of the polar ice.
But why do I imagine myself throned
Among such palaces of death and frost?

There is something strange and dreamlike
In returning after so many years:
The houses, the vegetation have grown
Familiar as if I saw them only yesterday.
Yet since I left here Youth has fled.
Still I have struggled on poor and alone.

*Mary Shelley*
*arranged by Brian Aldiss*

# Looking It Up

They praise your many interests,
Omniscient hierophant,
And how you make connections.
Yet this diversity suggests
That, much like Leacock's elephant,
You gallop off in all directions . . .

Yet how to make best sense?
For when I looked it up, of course,
I found that Jumbo was a horse,
And so my rhyme was wrecked.
We all need works of reference:
The brain's a fine and private place
But facts will slip from its embrace
(Though mysticism can't be checked).

# Rice Pudding

What is the matter with Mary Jane?
We hospital doctors stand round and complain
That the blip on her VDU's going insane.
What is the matter with Mary Jane?

What is the matter with Mary Jane?
We've analysed all her intestines contain
(Diced carrot, black pudding, and Chinese chow mein)
What is the matter with Mary Jane?

What is the matter with Mary Jane?
We've sunk our electrodes down into her brain;
I've tried two catheters, I've tried to explain.
 *But her bloody relations are weeping again* . . .

What is the matter with Mary Jane?
Among other things she has pre-menstrual pain.
(I guess that by now you'll recall the refrain:
What is the matter with Mary Jane?)

*Where*, by the way, is Mary Jane?
A nurse has already cracked under the strain:
The toilets and bedpans are filling in vain,
*Where*, by the way, is Mary Jane?

*Who*, incidentally, is Mary Jane?
She was nude when they carried her in from the rain.
Her driving licence was issued in *Spain* . . .
*Who*, incidentally, is Mary Jane?

What is the matter with Mary Jane?
She seems to want someone to entertain –
We're ringing Madonna, we've phoned Cleo Laine.
 *Now her bloody relations are weeping again* . . .

What is the matter with Mary Jane?
We've tried a heart transplant, X-rays, and methane,
And all the rest of the legerdemain.
What is the matter with Mary Jane?

What is the matter with Mary Jane?
I'll bet you my scalpel her life's on the wane —
She tried a U-turn in the M4 fast lane.
   *And her bloody relations are weeping again ...*

                                        *after A.A. Milne*

# Writer's Life

Playing unfashionable games,
Dreaming up unimaginable names,
Drinking coffee every hour,
Sitting watching the garden flower:
This is how a writer lives.

Waking in the middle of the night
Just to get a paragraph right,
Scribbling of wars, and saints, and turds,
Turning the whole world into words:
This is how a writer lives.

Waiting to get his agent's call,
Convinced he's the greatest writer of all,
Filling his computer full
Of lies both sad and beautiful
While courting Truth, austere and tall.
Preferring publishers to relations,
Attuned to unspoken conversations:
Dissatisfied, probably dissolute, depressed,
Partygoer, hermit, swank, strangely dressed,
Changer of the philistine world.
Jet-setter to New York and Japan,
Lover of phantoms, publicity-girled,
Lives like no one else can,
Dodges tax, sends fax after fax,
And, while life endures,
Enjoys the life-death parallax.
Knows some reviewers.

Late to bed, up about noon
Or maybe ten-thirty,
Likes to talk shop — or dirty —
Poems in his head, always a tune.
Watcher of ancient movies on the Box,
Wears odd socks. When on the rocks,

Sulks at the Groucho, dines at the Garrick,
Drinks Glenfiddich though doctor forbids.
Adores wife, likes life
(Has seven lives, four kids).
So a writer survives.

# IV  Scientific?

# Greenhouse Sex

Soon the greenhouse effect will emphasise
Drought, rain, winds, and shifting zones.
Though the population grows greyer
We greenhousers may never make old bones.

Northern Europe used to be reliable
Not least as regards sex and seduction.
Spring was the time. The lengthening days
Stimulated sex hormone production.

Northern animals developed breeding fettle
In springtime: May and mating linked.
Humans followed the pattern too.
Soon most of the animals will be extinct.

Sex was less programmed for tropic species.
For us too worse times now are waiting:
Inclement summers, intestinal complaints,
And a whole lot of intermittent mating.

# Lunar Anatomy

Blood is perpetually on the move
Clocking its orbits round the sun. Beneath
Grey Chinese soil lie limbs of those long dead
Awaiting live astronomers. And Hung-
Lsiang Chou has scrutinised femurs
Which date back over several thousand years
All carefully inscribed. Their runes record
Lunar eclipses of that distant age.

The days grow longer as our spiralling moon
Moon of mythology Earth's officer
Slowly absents herself. In Time's abyss
Before life stirred or flesh awoke a day
Died breathless in eight hours. Our sister then
Controlled the tides from narrow distances.

Diana huntress news of your desertion
Cries from computers and old Chinese bones.

# Monemvasia

An ocean without motion lies before us
Like life itself of which we are an instance,
While fading headlands in an Attic chorus
Give out the old news that there's always distance
Between the actual and what's desired,
Until the heart swells and the eye grows tired.

We take some photographs and move on soon:
To claim that we were here who now are gone.
We have a date in Athens, Sunday noon.
'We made it!' Yes, but timetables roll on.
A tamarisk bends to the southern air
As calendars rule tourists everywhere;

And yet a part of us is always free
And stands like Monemvasia, above
The storm – a goddess who, to some degree,
Shows both insight and blindness, born of love.
While Greece itself withstands the blast,
Symbol of liberty, of what must last.

Just as the olive trees flower forth from rock,
Mesembryanthemum and herb from dry cliff face,
So, though our scenes are set where much is stock,
Something within us seeks for unknown place,
For ruins which are inexpressible,
Springing from a time now inaccessible.

Evening! Sweet scents, and in the lower town
I wander many a crooked floral lane
Imagining as sober night comes down
Venetian, Byzant, Frank, alive again
To scheme and dream as I do, for a spell.
Then we retire to our one-star hotel.

Much as we try to purify our days
A ghost remains within a footstep's fall.
We too are part of what once was. Always,
That bird which sings by the taverna wall
Embraces time, cliffs, hopes and marjoram,
The Palaeologues, Byron, and Suleyman.

If joy is truly a true end of art
A visitor leaves here a better man.
If time is what has shaped all this in part
Is Ruin what an architect should plan? –
Just as some say our winter's evening
Is what we wished, unknowing, in our spring.

How comforting it is this hour to sleep
Among such ancient scenes! Lulled by their peace
The moon in the Aegean plunges deep.
The tumbled stonescapes of the Peloponnese
Receive her beams and, through the summer's night,
Themselves reflect a dim historic light.

# Found

Out of the primal universe are born
All elements except stability,
And we two creatures of that macro-storm
Are basking in our phase of parity
Before our atoms take up other bonds.
Wonderful that we have achieved the stature
To be whole! Ours is the strength that calms
The amniotic rivers of that first cohesion.
You come to me despite that dead small ghost,
Across your pallisades and worldly tenets,
Against all circumstance and transience.
And here we stand, no more among the lost,
Despite world fears, war, and the blood of planets –
What's that, my lady, if not high romance?

# Destruction of the Fifth Planet

Cool summer: mountains took on steeper angles
Smoke rose in clouds shaggy as forests
And consumed the earth
The great Mogu River disappeared
                                    screaming
Among the shuffled decks of strata
Then for a few days quiet
But the sun turned like a whirlpool till
All daylight ran with yellow sound
Eagles laboured against new winds
Finding that gravity was spiked with time
                                    And sulphurous smells

The animals on the fifth planet were various
A whistling thing which ran four-legged
With fur heavy as May blossom
Warbled a tune so luring that its prey
Could not but choose to follow and be killed.
Now that melodious death itself died
                                    In the general ash

Where ocean and beach were intermixed
A man ran with his beard alight
Calling and cursing to the stable stars

# Femalien

A waltz called Destiny
A town on far Arcturus
I met a lovely alien girl
Leading a brontosaurus.
The perspectives of that planet
Were puzzlingly vexatious
Yet so beautiful was she
I hoped for sexual relations.
She was willing but anatomy
Galactically grows complex
Her concave parts to shatter me
In every case were convex.

Thrilling the Alien is
But better stick to human
The proper study of mankind
            Is woman.

# Thomas Hardy Considers the Newly-Published
## Special Theory of Relativity

Doubtless there is a way of grasping whole
This troubled cosmos where we fare and die,
Of grasping, and forgiving much thereby.
   Well, some will chance, when I lie in the grave,
To quest like Albert Einstein for a key
   To ends so far obscured. Then let those brave
Unlock the universe's mystery,

Not I. If, with the Immanent Will's consent,
Mankind should gain some means to cancel space
And time, to view eternity's bleak face,
   Such vision could wreak endless dole – and fright
The human hopes of far futurity
   With woes yet stored, worse far than those which blight
Maids whom I know, and men who once knew me.

# 'Rhine Locks are Closed in Battle Against Poison'

*The Times* headline

Come on, it wasn't all that bad – the Dutch got windy!
Only a sunken sack of organophosphorous pesticide,
Only forty million fishes died:
Only the bloody ecologists made a shindy!

Only a four day scourge and then the usual formal
Notification that the poison had headed out to sea.
The German behaviour was exemplary:
Rhine pleasure-steamers carried on as normal.

# The Cat Improvement Company

We founded the Cat Improvement Co
For the betterment of the feline kind.
While taking their happiness to heart
We also had human good in mind.

As the blueprint shows, all those spikey teeth
Were requiring removal from tiny jaws.
To improve the symmetry of the whole
We decided against the whiskers and claws.

The morality, too, of the average cat
Could be definitely optimised straight away
By unwinding the helix of felix's genes
And blotting out some DNA.

The result is a quadruped bound to please,
All buttery soft and cushiony nice:
It pays no attention to moths or birds.
It has an abhorrence for catching mice.

Moreover, the Cat Improvement Co
Gives with each pet a guarantee:
'Outside bedroom windows it will not yowl;
Also in corners it will not pee.'

Ceaseless research moves forward yet
As we tackle the troublesome question of eyes:
What can be done to stop that glare
At spaces nothing occupies?

The CIC agenda shows
Updating is needed on silkier fur,
On gluttony, laziness, slinking,
And that aggravating purr.

The Perfect Cat is our ultimate aim
While, as far as technology reaches,
The HIC too is fulfilling its norms,
Improving the human species.

# The Expanding Universe

*Your wrist-watch ticks your mind away*
*The sons of men are slaves by birth*
*No soft untenanted green silence*
*Restores the murderer to earth*

But since my narrow science-tutored brain
Clings so tenaciously to what it learnt
In dusty boring schoolrooms, I believe
Still in the great expanding universe.

Another item of my faithless faith,
Contracted very likely from that same
Worn blackboard, is that space and time are one
Out there where space-time stretches like chewed string.

Why do I not then follow my belief
Or take an argosy beyond the sane? —
Where time like population swells and bursts
And propagates such mighty hours and days
That every minute holds a golden city
And lifetimes fail to fill one single second!

Look out for planets! cries the sun:
The skull responds with baby prattle:
The watched pot boils, while amputees
Prance on their stumps, dreaming of battle.

*Your wrist-watch ticks your mind away*
*The sons of men are slaves by birth*
*No soft untenanted green silence*
*Restores the murderer to earth*

# To a Triceratops Skull in the British Museum

Ah, you must have worn all that bone boldly
Right to the last hundred-ton headache

As from your snakeskin-shapeless egg you coldly
Invested your little all in cranial defences

Of course that poikilothermic ploy would drain
Energy from anything worth the name of brain

But you (your Self trapped in the osseous tunnel)
Lumber-rumbled out into the glowing

Late Jurassic world's hectic savannahs
To tup your mate with bugles blowing

# The Light

Jan had spent five long years
On the newly opened planet
Killing everything in sight.
Curious how on that last day,
Signing in his KZX-duster,
Climbing aboard the shuttle,
He turned for one last look
Before everything took flight –

And saw the tall trees like ginger
In the everlasting light.

# Flight 063

Why always speak of Icarus' fall? –
That legendary plunge
Amid a shower of tallow
And feathers and the poor lad's
Sweat? And that little splash
Which caught the eye of Brueghel
While the sun remained
Aloof within its private zone?

    That fall remains
Suspended in the corporate mind.
Yet as our Boeing flies
High above the Arctic Circle
Into the sun's eye, think –
Before the fall the flight was.
(So with Adam – just before
The Edenic Fall, he had
That first first taste of Eve.)

Dinner is served aboard Flight 063.
We eat from plastic trays, oblivious
To the stratosphere.

But Icarus – his cliff-top jump,
The leap of heart, the blue air scaled –
His glorious sense of life
Imperilled. Time
Fell far below, the everyday
Was lost in his ascent.

Up, up, he sailed, unheeding
Such silly limitations as
The melting point of wax.

# PRECARIOUS PASSIONS

## 1 A Brain Pursues its Vanished Dream

*Brain:*

Your fragrant presence haunts my sleeping—
The flower I pluck I find beyond my keeping . . .

Come back, don't leave! Among my labyrinths
   I found you wandering.
The sound of bells, a scent of hyacinths,
   A courtesan unknown,
Strangers, a doppelganger, woods, a king—
   All that you were is flown.
Stay! My erotic secret life sustain!
Return and dream yourself again.

*Dream:*

Dark in the mirror of your mind
   Deep in the wordless ways of Past
      Dear as a daughter lost for days
I bear my little lantern, blind
To sunlight, through the swamplands of
   Imagination.
      Curb your adoration.
      We shall not meet yet,
      Until Death holds you all aghast,
      And every tale is told.
My name is Sweet Regret.
   I flirt but I withold,
   And so you will erase
      My visitation.
       Love me and forget . . .

*She:*

Oh, what a nuptial is this!
You life-producing, hope-enhancing,
Winter-raging, summer-dancing
Mythic source of all my bliss.
   I give to you
   My being true –
You fill both heart and orifice!

*Ocean:*

Dream on, two legged fish,
With seaweed hair and painted face!
Dream on, and you may get your wish,
For thousands lie in my embrace,
Deep where no keel can ever trace.

*She:*

You scare me not. Love knows no fear.
You hope-enhancing, life-producing,
Summer-dancing, all-seducing,
Dynamo of all I do.
   Life I have got
   As you have not –
So I will drown myself in you.

# III Ascension Island Courts A Whale

*Island:*

Oh how alike we are in every way,
Both of us forging through the wide Atlantic,
The wise Atlantic, widow-making wild,
The broth of Earth, the breath of every day,
The stew of eons past and epochs antic—
*La mere*, of which I am, like you, a child . . .

Against your flanks as on my flanks there beat
Great waves that never knew a shore. And in
The fogs they bring, our love we'll consumate,
Hidden in our rock-bestrewn retreat.
I'll throw myself upon you and we'll sin
And sin again, and proudly procreate.

*Whale:*

I'm a shy sperm whale, and you don't realise
I'm heading for the sparkling southern seas,
And other islands . . . Mustn't be unkind—
I know you're lonely here—but can't disguise
The fact I have a Someone Else to please,
A old sweet isle—South Georgia's on my mind.

*Island:*

Come back, come back! The sea birds overhead
Bid me to burst from off my rocky bed,
And follow you where albatrosses fly.

*Whale:*

Your words are empty and your love is dead,
Dead as the lust your loneliness has fed.
Rise not, Ascension! Rest!
                            Good-bye!

                                Good-bye!

# iv A Refrigerator Proposes to a Musk Ox

*Musk ox:*

Stay back, you evil spirit, stay!
Beneath my hooves a mile of ice,
Above my back a mile of air,
Bearing the snows of Paradise —
    Just as my thoughts are choked with hay.

Stay back! I can discern it, you're
An iceberg's ghost in white attire,
Legless, armless, without pelt.
So melt — or say what you desire,
    You evil kitchen furniture.

*Refrigerator:*

As the aurora borealis glows
And flitters, let's enjoy sub-zero sex.
Look, I can open like a frosty rose!
My little button gleams in Greenland's dark.
Dear Musky, you're so hirsute I suppose
You're more than male. So don't be shy!
Just do what I propose.
Come hail, come storm!
    Mount me!

*Musk ox:*

                    It snows —
But since two months of night remain,
Whoppee! And here I come again . . .

## v A Book Falls in Love with its Reader

*Book:*

      O use your imagination!
How tenderly I felt your gaze
Myopic, probing, anodyne,
      Scan my pagination.
Over many days
      When I was in your clutch
I saw your lips move in praise!
To yield up each line
      Thrilled me so much
Beyond paraphrase.

      I'm sentenced to hint
That frankly your lover –
Though an Agatha Christie –
      Needs your imprint
From cover to cover.
      Now you're on the last chapter,
A climax indeed,
*O mine animal triste* . . .
      Repeat the fine rapture
And have a re-read!

*Reader:*

      Oh, I reciprocate your passion
And my heart's a true one,
For you are my gutenberg, my galaxy,
Right to the denouement.
I can't keep my eyes off you,
Other editions call in vain,
Throw off your wrapper
And I'll enter you again!

# VI A Lamp Standard Courts the Stars

*Lamp standard:*
> I'm not your humble supplicant,
>> Beset by piety and doubts:
>
> I am the sun of evening suburbs,
>> Ruler of routes and roundabouts,
>
> Great Inti of the interchange,
>> The Helios of all Highway Codes.
>
> I light the nomad and the northern towns,
>> The major mage of minor roads.

> In fog I burn when you go out,
>> My strength remains when yours declines,
>
> And yet – you're pretty little things,
>> So come and be my concubines.

*Stars:*
> What fun! Let's try, you frozen puffed-up thing!
> And welcome to our adamantine couch
> Where elementary particles all sing,
> And galaxies are forged and quarks debauch.
> They *switch you off* when dawn awakes:
> We're sempiternal, and what love we know
> Would melt you down to little sodium cakes!
> Come on, you night-light, then – let's go,
>> You microsecond gigolo!

# Alphabet of Ameliorating Hope

Angelic voices speak of a utopia which will soon come about
    once the secret research in Wisden, Ohio, is completed.

Basically, existence of a 'circumstance-chain' in human
    relationships will be established, proving causality
    between mental activity and the external physical
    world.

'Circumstance-chains' are operative in all human lives; for
    instance, the child deprived of love develops into a
    being who finds difficulty in establishing loving
    relationships in adulthood.

Directly the research is complete, we shall view the world
    anew.

Example: terms like 'loser' or 'the guy who has all the luck' will
    be seen as labels for those who are bound, favourably or
    otherwise, by circumstance-chains.

For clarity, this revolutionary new aspect of the human
    condition will be termed 'transpsychic reality'; a new
    sanity will prevail on earth.

Going mad will no longer be necessary.

Horror will vanish, fear will never strike.

Intellect will never more be scorned.

Joy will visit rich and poor alike.

Keeping faith in love and life will be an easier thing.

Love will not be just a theme that people sing.

Madge Winterbourne was the hero in Wisden, Ohio; she had originated the anti-catastrophe hypothesis.

No one who met her doubted she was the modern equivalent of a seer or saint.

Or an Einstein of the female sex.

Plans were hatched to release details of transpsychic reality to the whole world on the same day, the first of a new century.

Qualitative tests on volunteers in Wisden suggest that once people understand the pattern of their lives, they can be taught to take command of them.

Reality will then change; those who are malicious will see the root causes of the misery provoking their malice, and be able to expunge it.

Some criminals and power-seekers may prove more difficult to readjust, may indeed form a core of rebellion against the new utopia.

Transpsychic reality will see them gradually phased out.

Utopia, once on the move, will prove as irresistible as a glacier.

Very soon, a golden age – long dreamed of in the hearts and minds of men and women – will be established, which the animal kingdom will share with humans.

Wonder will grow like the cedar.

Xenophobia will die without voice.

You too will prevail, dear reader.

Zygotes themselves will rejoice.